WITHDRAWN

	DATE DUE		

Read All About *Horses*

LIPIZZANS

LYNN M. STONE

The Rourke Corporation, Inc.
Vero Beach, Florida 32964

ACKNOWLEDGEMENT:
The author thanks Tempel Farms, Wadsworth, IL, for its assistance and cooperation in the preparation of this book.

PHOTO CREDITS:
All photos © Lynn M. Stone except page 16 courtesy of Kentucky Horse Park

EDITORIAL SERVICES:
Penworthy Learning Systems

Library of Congress Cataloging-in-Publication Data

Stone, Lynn M.
    Lipizzans / Lynn M. Stone.
        p. cm. — (Horses)
    Includes index.
    Summary: Describes the history and physical characteristics of the horses known for their performances at the Spanish Riding School in Vienna, Austria.
    ISBN 0-86593-512-2
    1. Lipizzaner horse—Juvenile literature. [1. Lipizzaner horse. 2. Horses.] I. Title
II. Series: Stone, Lynn M. Horses.
SF293.L5S76 1998
636.1'38—dc21   98–25095
                                                                              CIP
                                                                              AC

Printed in the USA

TABLE OF CONTENTS

LIPIZZANS

The Lipizzan is a rare and strikingly beautiful **breed** (BREED), or type, of horse. Lipizzans are almost always white or light gray when they are adults. They are generally used as riding horses or to pull carriages.

As riding horses, the most talented Lipizzans are trained to perform amazing moves in a show ring. Many of these movements are part of a traditional riding style called **dressage** (dreh SAHJH).

Lipizzans were named for the village of Lipiza in Slovenia. The breed was first developed there.

A Lipizzan mare pauses from her breakfast in a spring-green pasture.

THE FIRST LIPIZZANS

The Lipizzan breed is from an area that was once part of Austria. The Lipizzan's bloodlines, though, are largely Spanish.

Lipizzans like these at Tempel Farms in northern Illinois have been bred in Austria for more than 400 years.

Frisky in the morning sun, a Lipizzan stallion gallops about his paddock.

Spanish horses were imported by Austria in 1580. Those horses and their offspring became the chosen horses of nobles at the Spanish Riding School in Vienna. They also became some of the ancestors of modern Lipizzans.

The breed continued to develop in the 1700s. Spanish horses from Italy, Denmark, and Germany were crossed with the Austrian horses.

LIPIZZAN HISTORY

In 1816, the horse **breeders** (BREE derz) introduced Arabian blood into their Lipizzan stock. That improved the breed even more.

In the final days of World War II, however, the Lipizzan breed nearly met disaster. Many of the best horses were kept in Vienna, at the Spanish Riding School. In March, 1945, the war moved dangerously close. With great difficulty the horses were moved safely to Saint Martin.

The American army soon returned the horses to Vienna. Lipizzans still perform in Vienna's great old Riding Hall. Lipizzans have performed there since 1735.

Lipizzans enjoy a morning romp, but the handsome Lipizzan is prized for performing, not speed.

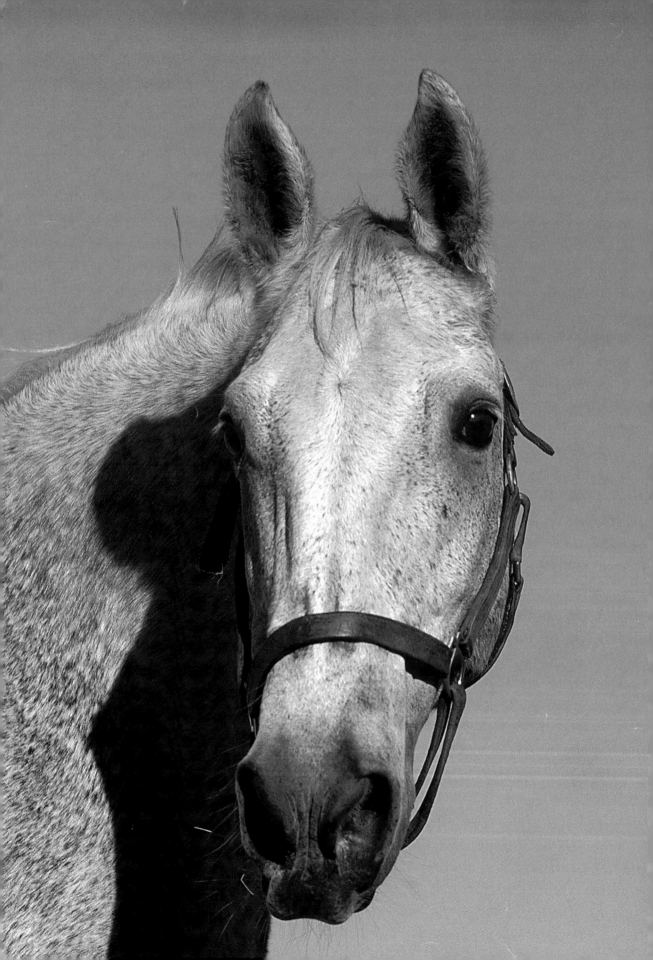

LIPIZZANS IN AMERICA

Lipizzans are well known to horse lovers because of their beauty and talent. But Lipizzans are a rare breed. The world population is probably no more than 3,000 **purebred** (PEUR bred) Lipizzans. In the United States, there are perhaps 400 purebreds.

American Lipizzans are kept mainly for their talent as performers. At the Tempel Farms in northern Illinois, Lipizzans perform in the same manner as those at the Spanish Riding School. Over a million visitors have watched the Tempel Lipizzans perform.

A rare breed of horse, Lipizzans only number about 400 purebred animals in the United States.

THE LIPIZZAN BODY

The Lipizzan has a compact, well-formed body. It has a long head, usually with the nose slightly arched. It has small ears, a deep, wide chest, and strong, muscular legs.

Still the color of soot, this young Lipizzan stallion will become white with age.

Two young Lipizzans take a moment to horse around.

   Although most Lipizzans are white, or nearly so, a few are black or a shade of brown. The Lipizzan **stallions** (STAL yunz), or male horses, used for performing are always white or light gray.
   Lipizzans stand 15 to 16 **hands** (HANDZ) (about five feet or two meters) at the shoulders. A full-grown Lipizzan weighs up to 1,200 pounds (545 kilograms).

THE LIPIZZAN FOAL

A Lipizzan **foal** (FOL) weighs about 120 pounds (55 kilograms) at birth. It grows quickly on its mother's milk and soon begins to mix its milk diet with grass and hay. By the time it's five months old, the foal no longer nurses.

Curiously, Lipizzan foals are brown or dark gray. The coats of almost all Lipizzans, however, slowly lighten as the horses age. Some Lipizzans aren't white until they're 10-year-olds.

A Lippizan foal begins wearing a halter (strap around the face) when it's just three days old.

GROWING UP A LIPIZZAN

In the **tradition** (truh DISH un), or way, of the Spanish Riding School, only Lipizzan stallions perform. Serious training begins at four years. A trainer works young stallions at the end of a long rein. In that way the trainer studies a horse's ability.

Young female horses, called **fillies** (FIL eez), are usually trained for pulling carriages or pleasure riding. Some Lipizzan mares, the adult female horses, are used mainly to produce new foals.

Only Lipizzan stallions are used for performances, in the tradition of the old Spanish Riding School in Vienna, Austria.

LIPIZZANS AT WORK

As harness horses, some Lipizzans are trained to pull carriages. In Europe, the Lipizzan is commonly used for this purpose.

Kindness from the trainer helps bring out the talent of the intelligent Lipizzan.

Even out of the ring, a Lipizzan stallion is a study of beauty and graceful movement.

The most talented Lipizzan stallions are riding horses, trained to perform very demanding moves. In one such move, the stallion makes several forward jumps using only his hind, or back, legs. In another, the horse leaps into the air and kicks out his hind legs.

Stallions are also taught to perform at the end of a long rein without a rider.

THE LIPIZZAN'S COUSINS

The Arab is a close relative of the Lipizzan. The Arab is an older breed than the Lipizzan, and it was used to improve early Lipizzan stock. The Arab, or Arabian, is known for its beauty, intelligence, and endurance—the ability not to tire easily.

Arabians tend to be fairly small, standing under five feet (one and a half meters) at the shoulder.

The Arab comes in many colors, from dark to white. Lipizzan breeders in 1816 used a white Arabian stallion.

Another handsome, graceful horse, the Arab was an early ancestor of the Lipizzan.

GLOSSARY

breed (BREED) — a particular group of domestic animals having the same characteristics, such as shape or color

breeder (BREE der) — one who raises animals, such as horses, and lets them reproduce

dressage (dreh SAHJH) — complex moves by a horse in response to a rider's shifting weight

filly (FIL ee) — a young female horse

foal (FOL) — a horse before the age of one year

hand (HAND) — a four-inch (ten-centimeter) measure of horses' shoulder height

purebred (PEUR bred) — a domestic, or tame, animal of a single (pure) breed

stallion (STAL yun) — an adult male horse that can father foals

tradition (truh DISH un) — an event done in the same way now that it has always been done

Dark for now, this Lipizzan foal will most likely turn white by the time it's six or seven years old.

INDEX

FURTHER READING

Find out more about horses with these helpful books and organizations:
Clutton-Brock, Juliet. *Horse.* Knopf, 1992.
Edwards, Elwyn H. *The Encyclopedia of the Horse.* Dorling Kindersley, Inc., 1994.
Hendricks, Bonnie. *International Encyclopedia of Horse Breeds.* University of
   Oklahoma, 1995.